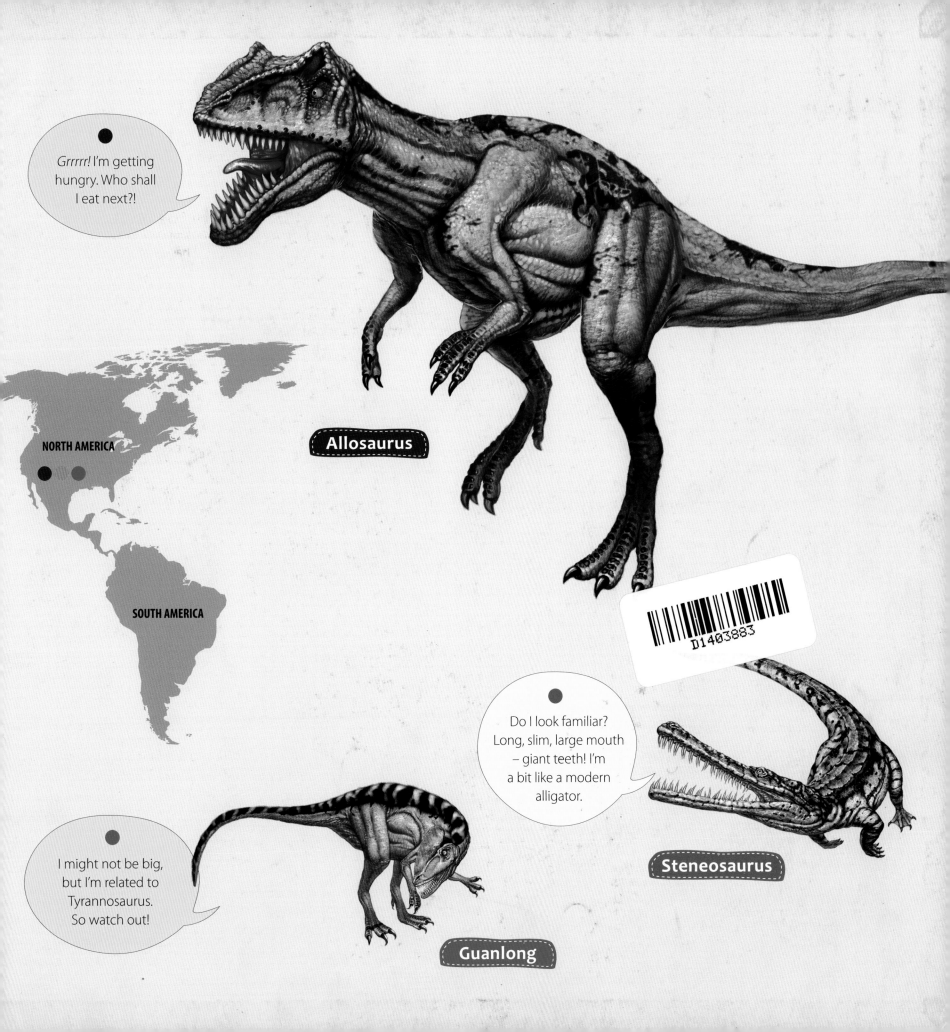

big & SMALL

Original Korean text and illustrations by Dreaming Tortoise
Korean edition © Aram Publishing

This English edition published by big & SMALL in 2016
by arrangement with Aram Publishing
English text edited by Scott Forbes
English edition © big & SMALL 2016

Distributed in the United States and Canada by
Lerner Publishing Group, Inc.
241 First Avenue North
Minneapolis, MN 55401 U. S. A.
www.lernerbooks.com

Photo credits:
Page 29, middle: © Ghedoghedo;
bottom: © Kabacchi

To learn about dinosaur fossils, see page 28.
For information on the main groups of dinosaurs,
see the Dinosaur Family Tree on page 30.

Rampaging
Allosaurus

Allosaurus

big & SMALL

Utahraptor

Snarling and hissing, the four Utahraptors
closed in on a young Iguanodon.
Using their powerful back legs,
they leaped high onto its back.
Then they slashed and ripped
with their long, hooked claws.

IGUANODON

GROUP: Ornithopods
DIET: Plants
WHEN IT LIVED: Early Cretaceous
WHERE IT LIVED: North America (USA),
Asia (Mongolia), Europe (UK, Germany),
Africa (Tunisia)
LENGTH: 20–36 feet (6–11 meters)
HEIGHT: 16.5 feet (5 meters)
WEIGHT: 3.3–6.6 tons
(3–6 tonnes)

6

Utahraptor's curved claws help it grab and kill its prey. The name "Utahraptor" means "hunter of Utah." Utah is the name of the state in America where fossils of this dinosaur were first found.

HEIGHT: 6.6 feet (2 meters)

LENGTH: 20–23 feet (6–7 meters)

WEIGHT: 0.55–9.5 tons (0.5–0.85 tonnes)

WHEN IT LIVED: TRIASSIC JURASSIC CRETACEOUS

GROUP: Theropods

DIET: Meat

WHERE IT LIVED: North America (USA)

Although it was large, Utahraptor was quite light, which helped it move quickly. Utahraptors usually hunted in groups, known as packs. That way they could catch prey much larger than themselves. Once they had selected their target, they surrounded it. Then they attacked from all sides.

Losing strength, the Iguanodon crashed to the ground with a thud. The victorious Utahraptors swarmed on top of it. Now they would enjoy a great feast.

Hypsilophodon

SAY IT:
Hip-sih-LOH-foh-don

Three Hypsilophodons were feeding on small shrubs.
Even as they ate, they were alert for signs of danger.
All at once they heard the thudding of heavy footsteps.
Were they under attack?

Hypsilophodon was a gentle dinosaur.
It lived in groups and fed on low-growing plants.
It had a mouth like a parrot's beak.
Inside were sharp front teeth for cutting off leaves
and many fan-shaped teeth for chewing.

HEIGHT: 1.6–4 feet
(0.5–1.2 meters)

LENGTH: 6.6–8 feet
(2–2.5 meters)

WEIGHT: 66–150 pounds
(30–70 kilograms)

WHEN IT LIVED: TRIASSIC | JURASSIC | CRETACEOUS

GROUP: Ornithopods

DIET: Plants

WHERE IT LIVED:
North America (USA),
Europe (UK, Portugal),
Asia (Korea)

A fearsome Deinonychus had its eye on them.
The Hypsilophodons saw it coming toward
them, baring its sharp teeth.
In an instant, they turned and darted
through the undergrowth at top speed,
powering along on their strong hind legs.

Hypsilophodon could run as fast as a car on a highway.
So even though Deinonychus was a fast runner,
it could not keep up with this speedy plant-eater!

DEINONYCHUS

GROUP: Theropods
DIET: Meat
WHEN IT LIVED: Early Cretaceous
WHERE IT LIVED: North America (USA)
LENGTH: 10–12 feet (3–3.5 meters)
HEIGHT: 4 feet (1.2 meters)
WEIGHT: 175–220 pounds
(80–100 kilograms)

Archaeopteryx

SAY IT:
Ar-kay-OP-ter-icks

Standing perfectly still, an Archaeopteryx stared at the forest floor and waited. Soon, a little lizard scuttled across the sand. The Archaeopteryx silently spread its wings. Then — *whoosh!* — it swooped and snapped up the tiny creature. That's one tasty snack for Archaeopteryx!

LENGTH: 1–1.7 feet (30–50 centimeters)

HEIGHT: 8–12 inches (20–30 centimeters)

WEIGHT: 2–6.5 pounds (1–3 kilograms)

WHEN IT LIVED:	TRIASSIC	JURASSIC	CRETACEOUS

GROUP: Theropods	DIET: Meat (insects)

WHERE IT LIVED: Europe (Germany)

The name "Archaeopteryx" means "wings of ancient times." It was one of the first feathered dinosaurs to be found. It helped scientists understand that birds are related to dinosaurs.

Archaeopteryx was quite different from modern birds. For instance, it had sharp teeth inside its beak and it had fingers and hooked claws on its wings.

Allosaurus

An Allosaurus had been resting in the shade. But now it was time to eat. It had spotted an Apatosaurus nearby and got ready to attack it.

Allosaurus was almost as large and fierce as Tyrannosaurus. And even though it was big and heavy, it could move quickly on its strong legs.

16

APATOSAURUS

GROUP: Sauropods
DIET: Plants
WHEN IT LIVED: Late Jurassic
WHERE IT LIVED: North America
(USA, Canada)
LENGTH: 62–82 feet (19–25 meters)
HEIGHT: 16.5 feet (5 meters)
WEIGHT: 27–31 tons
(25–28 tonnes)

HEIGHT: **10–13 feet**
(3–4 meters)
LENGTH: **25–40 feet**
(7.5–12 meters)
WEIGHT: **1.6–3.3 tons**
(1.5–3 tonnes)

WHEN IT LIVED:	TRIASSIC	JURASSIC	CRETACEOUS
GROUP: **Theropods**		DIET: **Meat**	

WHERE IT LIVED:
North America (USA),
Europe (Portugal),
Africa (Tanzania), Australia

Allosaurus had a massive head, powerful jaws, and rows of long, sharp teeth. It ate almost any living thing it could catch. When it couldn't find live prey, it feasted on dead animals.

Two long bony ridges ran from Allosaurus's snout up to the top of its head, forming two triangular bumps above its eyes.

Suddenly a Ceratosaurus appeared in front of the
Allosaurus. It had its eye on the Apatosaurus too.
The Allosaurus flew at it and knocked it to the ground.
The Ceratosaurus struggled to its feet then dashed away,
into nearby bushes. It was no match for Allosaurus!

CERATOSAURUS

GROUP: Theropods
DIET: Meat
WHEN IT LIVED: Late Jurassic
WHERE IT LIVED: Africa (Tanzania),
North America (USA)
LENGTH: 20–33 feet (6–10 meters)
HEIGHT: 8 feet (2.5 meters)
WEIGHT: 1.1 tons
(1 tonne)

Steneosaurus

A Steneosaurus swam swiftly through the shallow water. *Snap!* It grabbed a tasty-looking fish in its massive jaws.

Steneosaurus looked like today's crocodiles and alligators. It was about the same size, but its jaws were a little longer and narrower.

Steneosaurus lived mainly in the sea, but it sometimes swam into rivers. Its mouth was an ideal shape for scooping fish up in the water.

PLESIOSAURUS

GROUP: Ichthyosaurs
DIET: Meat (fish)
WHEN IT LIVED: Early Jurassic
WHERE IT LIVED: Europe (UK, Germany)
LENGTH: 10–16.5 feet (3–5 meters)
HEIGHT: 16 inches (40 centimeters)
WEIGHT: 0.5 tons
(0.45 tonnes)

Steneosaurus was an amphibian. That means it could swim in the water and walk on land. But because it could only walk slowly, Steneosaurus preferred to stay in the water, where it could move much more quickly.

Steneosaurus often lay in the water with only its nostrils above the surface. This allowed it to breathe while remaining out of sight.

HEIGHT: 16 inches (40 centimeters)

LENGTH: 10–16.5 feet (3–5 meters)

WEIGHT: 290 pounds (130 kilograms)

WHEN IT LIVED: TRIASSIC | JURASSIC | CRETACEOUS

GROUP: Teleosaurids

DIET: Meat

WHERE IT LIVED: Europe (UK, Germany, France, Switzerland), Africa (Morocco)

Guanlong

SAY IT:
GWAN-long

24

A group of Guanlongs were hunting for prey. Two were chasing giant dragonflies. Another was following a tiny lizard. It tried to snatch it up. The lizard scuttled out of its reach, but then ran straight into another Guanlong, which quickly speared it with its sharp front claws.

HEIGHT: **3.3 feet**
(1 meter)

LENGTH: **10 feet**
(3 meters)

WEIGHT: **165–220 pounds**
(75–100 kilograms)

WHEN IT LIVED: | **TRIASSIC** | **JURASSIC** | **CRETACEOUS**

GROUP: **Theropods**   DIET: **Meat**

WHERE IT LIVED:
Asia (China)

Guanlong had a large crest on its head. Adult male Guanlongs used their crest to attract a mate.

Guanlong was a fairly small dinosaur, with a small head and long feet with three toes. But it was fierce and could move quickly.

Scientists think Guanlong was an early ancestor of Tyrannosaurus.

Guanlongs were not large enough to hunt big dinosaurs like Mamenchisaurus. But groups of Guanlongs would follow Mamenchisaurus families, keeping a close watch on the young ones. If any baby Mamenchisaurus moved away from their parents, the Guanlongs would pounce.

MAMENCHISAURUS

GROUP: Sauropods
DIET: Plants
WHEN IT LIVED: Late Jurassic
WHERE IT LIVED: Asia (China, Mongolia)
LENGTH: 72–80 feet (22–25 meters)
HEIGHT: 25 feet (7.6 meters)
WEIGHT: 22–28 tons (20–25 tonnes)

Dinosaur Fossils

Fossils are the remains of dinosaurs. They can be hard parts of dinosaurs, such as bones and teeth, that have slowly turned to stone. Or they may be impressions of bones, teeth, or skin preserved in rocks.

▶ Utahraptor's extra-large claw

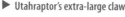

Utahraptor

When fossils of Utahraptor were first found in 1975, the discovery didn't attract much attention. But, in 1991, scientists found an extremely large claw from the same dinosaur. It was the biggest claw yet found from the dinosaurs called raptors. Since then, however, even bigger raptor claws have been located, including those of much larger relatives like Gigantoraptor and Sinraptor.

Hypsilophodon

When Hypsilophodon fossils were first discovered, in 1984, scientists thought they were those of a young Iguanodon. But later finds revealed that they belonged to a dinosaur that was quite different from Iguanodon. Unlike Iguanodon, Hypsilophodon was small, made nests, stood guard over its eggs and young, and lived in large groups.

▲ Model of Hypsilophodon skeleton

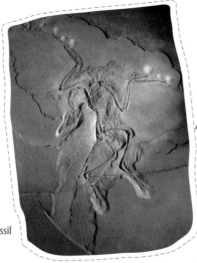

▶ Model of Archaeopteryx fossil

Archaeopteryx

The first Archaeopteryx fossil was dug up in Solnhofen, Germany, in 1859. It was found in layers of limestone, a rock that preserves fossils well. Ten more Archaeopteryx fossils were soon found in the same area, one after another. The patterns of these dinosaurs' feathers were clearly visible in the rocks.

Allosaurus

▲ Model of Allosaurus skull

It took some time to put together a complete picture of Allosaurus. Small fossils were discovered in Colorado, USA, in 1877, but provided few clues as to what this dinosaur was like. Then, in 1927, the remains of several Allosaurus were found in a swamp. This allowed scientists to piece together a whole skeleton and get a clearer idea of how this fearsome dinosaur looked, lived, and hunted.

Steneosaurus

Steneosaurus fossils were among the earliest reptile fossils to be found, in 1825, in Germany. The fossils showed that Steneosaurus had scales on its back and stomach. This suggested that it lived at least part of the time in water. In fact, the long mouth and sharp teeth of Steneosaurus were very similar to those of a modern alligator found in India, called the garial.

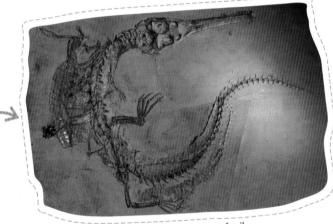

▲ Model of Steneosaurus fossil

Guanlong

▶ Guanlong fossil

It was a Chinese-American research team that discovered the first Guanlong fossil, in 2006. The dinosaur's name was chosen in 2011. In Chinese it means "lizard with a crown," which refers to the crest on the dinosaur's nose. Sometimes it is also called the "five-colored crowned lizard" because it was discovered near rocks of five different colors.

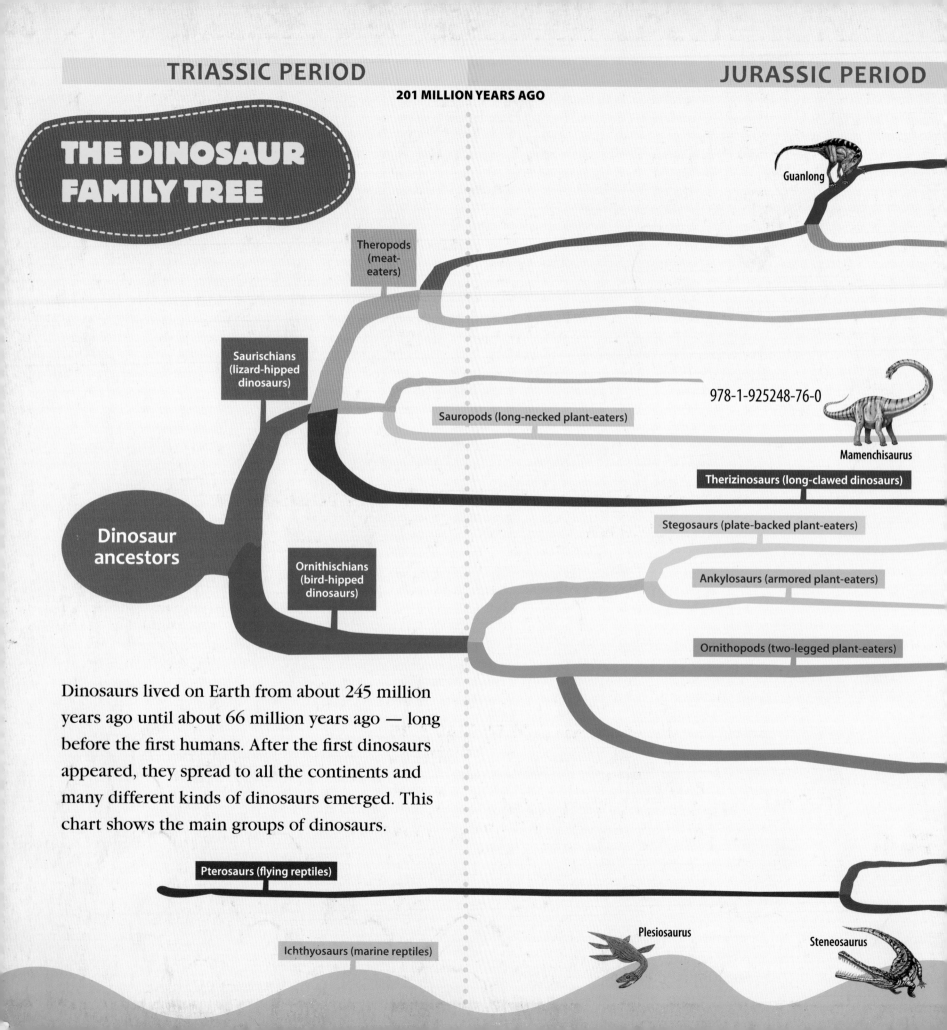

201 MILLION YEARS AGO

THE DINOSAUR FAMILY TREE

Guanlong

Theropods (meat-eaters)

Saurischians (lizard-hipped dinosaurs)

Sauropods (long-necked plant-eaters)

978-1-925248-76-0

Mamenchisaurus

Therizinosaurs (long-clawed dinosaurs)

Stegosaurs (plate-backed plant-eaters)

Dinosaur ancestors

Ankylosaurs (armored plant-eaters)

Ornithischians (bird-hipped dinosaurs)

Ornithopods (two-legged plant-eaters)

Dinosaurs lived on Earth from about 245 million years ago until about 66 million years ago — long before the first humans. After the first dinosaurs appeared, they spread to all the continents and many different kinds of dinosaurs emerged. This chart shows the main groups of dinosaurs.

Pterosaurs (flying reptiles)

Plesiosaurus

Steneosaurus

Ichthyosaurs (marine reptiles)